The American Dream

A Personal and Professional Leadership Journey

by

Andres Gutierrez, P.Eng., PMP

Andres Gutierrez

To you, I just start off by saying…

Great things have been accomplished by people who TRUST in God and BELIEVE they can accomplish them.

Acknowledgements

Give me a place to stand and I will move the earth!
~Archimedes

It is said that behind every great man there is a great woman, and I could not agree more, but I must add that behind every man there is a great family as well.

I want to thank my oldest daughter, Laura, and my son, Ian, for being that powerful engine that keeps me going to the speed and intensity that I go. Without you guys I would not be who I am now; I am proud of you both. To my two youngest daughters, Ella and Natalie, thank you for bringing to my life happiness and joy – you guys showed me how important it is to dream and be crazy. And to my wife Lyndsey, thank you for your unconditional love and the support that makes the impossible possible.

To my grandmother and mother, Luz and Mery, your personal stories are unbelievable, and they are a true testimony of humbleness and believing. Your humility and dedication shaped my personality and gave me a different perspective of life when I see the world.

You all *give me a place to stand so I can continue to move the earth.* I love you all!

I also want to acknowledge how thankful I am to all those I have had the opportunity to work with, both personally and professionally. You all mentored me in one way or another and helped build the leadership skills I needed to advance in my career and profession.

You know who you are. Again, a big thank you for all you have done and continue to do for me.

Table of Contents

Introduction 7
Chapter 1: **A Place I Once Called Home** 12
Chapter 2: **The Decision** 21
Chapter 3: **The United States** 28
Chapter 4: **An American dream** 36
Chapter 5: **Canada** 43
Chapter 6: **A Professional Path** 49
Chapter 7: **The Plan** 60
Chapter 8: **A New Door Opens** 69
Chapter 9: **Mentorship** 77
Chapter 10: **Why Be Complacent?** 88
Chapter 11: **New Challenges** 95
Chapter 12: **My Secret and My True Dream** 102

Introduction

It is said that one thing an individual must do in his or her lifetime is write a book and tell a compelling story from which someone else could benefit. Well, it is now 10:08 a.m. on a beautiful, cold winter morning: the perfect time to start writing down what I experienced while facing the unknown. I left behind a place I once called home to face a challenging journey, moving to a new country I did not know anything about, and resetting my career path by jumping into a world of challenging and exciting obstacles.

The main message in this book is about that: discovering the strengths you may not know you have or the weaknesses you do not want to acknowledge; becoming a true leader; belonging and succeeding in your pursuits of happiness wherever you are or go, regardless of the circumstances around you; finding the motivation required to overcome challenging situations; and achieving personal and professional success.

THE AMERICAN DREAM

There are so many people feeling unfulfilled with what they have accomplished in life thus far, questioning their current situation as students, professionals, parents, sons, daughters, etc. They are questioning their life in general; thinking of giving themselves another opportunity to start all over again and having a new or even a last chance to offer themselves, their families and future generations, a better future; a future in a country where it is said that money overflows and where there are opportunities everywhere.

Some other people, successful and not that successful, just want to avoid the questions that will probably bother them for the rest of their lives:

> *What would have happened if I had made the decision to...? Where would I be now if I had done it or gone there, when I had the chance?*

and so forth…

Well, that was my case, and I finally made the decision to share my experiences with all those going through any of these circumstances, the ones who had already made it across and conquered the Canadian or American dream. Why not share my journey with all who, somehow, have the control over key situations and decisions that can change the future and destiny of newcomers or new generations to come?

Over the years, friends, family members and even slight acquaintances have approached me seeking advice when they need to make a critical decision that may affect others, especially those close to them. Based on their positive outcomes and in my own experience, I want to represent through this book, events, facts and actual situations that led me to where I am now: living a comfortable and happy life – living my dream.

With passion I can also say that I have accomplished so much since I left my comfort zone and decided to leave the place I once called home; with that very same passion I have to say that there is so much ahead to accomplish. I will continue to set more personal and professional goals, challenging myself to work smarter and harder to accomplish the unthinkable.

As a matter of fact, this my first advice: if you are thinking of leaving your comfort zone and you believe that it would be easy to move on in your career path or improve your financial situation, in a new country or company without any effort and relying only on your luck or the people you think you

THE AMERICAN DREAM

know – you could already be making the first mistake.

A non-complacency mindset is also key. Canada or the United States can bring you very easily to a comfort level where you do not need to go that extra mile to live a decent life. In Canada for instance, there are many social assistance agencies, government programs for foreign-trained professionals, community centers, religious organizations and other groups where help and guidance may be found. But to excel in what you do best, only that non-complacency mentality, along with positive thinking and realistic goals, can help you overcome every obstacle ahead of you in your new adventures.

Fortunately, Canada, and believe it or not, the United States, are two of the very few countries in the world that open their doors to people going through adversity in life, as well as to qualified and skillful professionals.

In the case of Canada, multiculturalism is embraced to its full potential. This is a great advantage that cannot be found anywhere else. In the USA, the pride of every state for their own customs, traditions and beliefs is admirable and adopted by all.

Andres Gutierrez

Imagine people from all over the world getting together in a single city – Latin Americans, Asians, Middle Easterners, Europeans, Africans; the mix of all these cultures, their food, background, religion, dress codes, their successes or failures, all get combined and exposed on every street and public place for everyone to see, enjoy and learn from. All of them trying to show off where they are coming from without hesitation, showing everyone what they are made of. Even the ancestors of Canadian and American first generations did the same when they first came over years ago, leaving behind discrimination, oppression, and violence. In some other cases they decided to embark on a new journey just to explore and conquer a new world; making of Canada or the United States what they are right now.

All the history behind our beautiful new country, its present and especially its future, makes me look back to the very same moment where I made the decision to leave home; to thank God for putting in my mind the thought of pursuing my Dream.

Chapter One

A Place I Once Called Home

Success is not a coincidence; it is part of any starving professional! ~Anonymous

It is great feeling to have a professional degree! After so many years at a post-secondary school preparing ourselves for a better future, we are now approaching graduation day and the time where we will apply all that acquired knowledge in the job market and, of course, contribute to society. Everyone is excited.

Finally the time when we start making real money is upon us, even for those of us who have been thinking ahead and trying to land a potential job before school is done. The future is a mystery for everyone; all we have to start with in our new journey is the advice we received from family members and friends, seeing through their eyes and perspectives what it is like to be employed and making a decent living.

Most of us are the first generation in our families to obtain a professional degree, and the future does not look promising for some. A few others, those with better luck and connections, are already making their way into big corporations and global companies. Now the question is, what are the ones without that "luck" going to do now?

The answer is simple: they can bring the job requirements of a taxi cab driver or a janitorial or grocery store associate to the next level, right?

We all share the same thoughts and were afraid of spending so many years at school finishing university just to end up unemployed or having to work in a different field from what we studied. We begin to imagine the disappointment we will bring to ourselves and our families if we cannot find something close to the expectations.

Mom and Dad sacrificed so much to pay for our education and now they expect, in an indirect way, to be paid back just by knowing that our future will be better than their own present. In other cases, they believe that providing a good quality education

THE AMERICAN DREAM

to their children in the present is a way to be financially secure in the future. *This is the most common way parents in a Third World country plan and secure their retirement years.*

Speaking of the differences between a First and a Third World country, here is a major economic gap between the two of them – in the former, post-secondary education is pretty much a choice, while it is a privilege that not everyone has in the latter.

> The desire to excel and knowing what obstacles you need to overcome are the first steps to pursuing a successful life.

Government grants, student loans, and possibly family funds are among the choices given to young people in the First World to start the educational foundation needed to make a difference in the workforce and secure their future lives. Nevertheless, most people in a developed country opt to work and go to school at the same time. This is the sociocultural behavior of individuals in a First World country once high school is completed. Young people are not afraid of working while fulfilling the commitments of post-secondary education. Hard work is already embedded in most individuals; that is how they are raised.

Back where I grew up, the relaxed lifestyle and "going with flow" mindset were some of the diseases that affected promising young individuals. You can prove that you want to make a difference by not following that path. The desire to excel and knowing what obstacles you need to overcome are the first steps to pursuing a successful life. That is what I did, and now you and I have that in common. Despite the easy choices given to us, we decided to challenge ourselves with a higher level of personal objectives. *Well done!*

Being proactive helped me land my first job. Through a family friend connection, I was able to join a small-sized food processing company for an internship opportunity. Even though the pay was not that much – just enough to cover transportation fares and my basic necessities – I considered myself fortunate to find something before school was finished. Sadly, most of my classmates struggled to even get a phone interview for potential employment.

I will never forget the feeling of being employed for the first time and knowing that this was the beginning of my career. But being a recent graduate, new to a company and lacking experience, I

THE AMERICAN DREAM

was quickly introduced to the real world and what it is like to start from the bottom. Some of us believed that just having a professional degree was a first class ticket into a big role in a corporation.

A year and a half down the road, working extra time, commuting from a small town to the big city for more than three hours every day, and trying to make ends meet at the end of each month, made me wonder what spending five years of my time at school had been for.

School was finished at this point, and with my enthusiastic mentality I convinced myself that I could ask my managers to consider me for a better job. In fact, there was a great opportunity ahead of me: I learned that the person I reported to was being promoted to a higher managerial position within the company and I knew that I could actually backfill the manager role.

In no time the excitement overtook me. I spent sleepless nights thinking of ideas to impress the company's leadership team and make this opportunity the foundation of a bright professional future. After I had expressed to my manager my interest in the position, days, weeks and months passed by without hearing back anything about recruiting arrangements or even an internal job posting. My excitement was turning to anxiety until I heard from guys working on the shop floor that a close friend of the plant manager was going to take over the role I had been waiting for. I felt as if someone had hit me with a baseball bat, and I started to feel sick to my stomach.

> *Well, the good news is that at least I still have a job, eh?*

That was not the mentality I had; of course, it took time to mentally recalibrate myself and come up with a new plan. I was not going to spend the rest of my life working behind the scenes. My youth and ambition put a thought into my head: I had to work harder, contribute directly to the success of the area I was part of and exceed everyone's expectations. At the end of the day, that was why I had gone to school and prepared myself for so many years.

Having been raised by my grandparents – my mother's parents – and knowing very little about my father, I decided to do a little bit of research on my dad's side of the family. I did not want to reach out directly to him as I remembered my mom and grandmother asking him for help when I was a little boy, and always being turned down with the same phrase:

THE AMERICAN DREAM

Leave me alone, I did not get any help when I was growing up. I am certain you guys can manage.

I also remembered that when I was about ten or twelve years old I had met a distant uncle. I recalled my grandmother having a conversation with him about work and completing his university studies. Through a neighbor's contact, I got his phone number and after several phone calls I finally got hold of him. Without hesitation he recommended me for a supervisory position at one of the companies he worked for as a consultant. *Connections, connections, connections!!!*

I remember having my first real job interview for that supervisor position. During the initial interview session, the area leader was very tough and did not care where my resume was coming from. Her point was that I had the education but not the experience required to replace a 35-year senior employee. So many years of service without major contributions to the company and an old-school managerial style were the main reasons he was being forced to retire – in other words, let go. They needed new ideas and a new set of eyes for the role as the company was growing rapidly, and they were not able to keep up with the workload.

During the interview process I just kept telling myself not to let the opportunity go away. Then I realized that the only way to change the interviewer's predisposed mentality and lack-of-experience perception of me was by answering the questions with statements and phrases she wanted to hear.

Here is a simple example I hope you can relate to or learn from:

Area Manager:

Being so young, how are you going to give orders to employees with more than 25 years of experience, who do not seem to listen or care about anything?

Since I was relatively new to the workplace environment, to me there was not any difference between a 2 or 50-year senior employee.

And my answer was:

It's not about giving orders. In my opinion it is about communication. Communication is key in any corporation nowadays. It does not matter where in the world you are, all employees would like to feel that they are being heard, counted on and that their ideas are important. That is why, when it comes to a

> *culture of change, the employees need to believe that the so called "change" is coming from their suggestions and ideas, not from someone else.*

Years later, I came to realize how true my statement was.

Right away I noticed how the facial expressions and gestures of the area manager changed in a positive manner. I decided to switch the interview process the other way around, and I began to ask some questions about the company and the expectations they had for the role, not giving the interviewer the opportunity, in a polite way, to catch me off guard with an unexpected question. After that, I focused two or three more questions on her. It turned out that she had gone to the same university as I had and even pursued the same professional degree I have. Somehow, she connected herself with me, and the rest is now history.

Chapter Two

The Decision

The decisions we make throughout our lifetime will become the path that leads us to our ultimate destination. Think and act wisely. ~AG

Being a young person working as an area supervisor leading a group of senior employees was my first experience dealing with real-life situations and people behavior issues. As time passed I got well versed in the company's processes and got to know my people. The concepts that I brought to the workplace were difficult to

> It is now in my blood to have a non-complacency mindset and constantly seek personal growth.

accept for some employees reporting to me, and I finally began to face the challenges I had signed up for. Of course, they did not want to change what they had been doing for so many years.

I was challenged in all my attempts to do my job, to the point where I began to believe that I did not have any authority or credibility when proposing and implementing new ideas. I did not know what to do about the whole situation. My attempt to perform well was strategically designed to impress my manager and show the company's upper management team how eager I was to excel and make it into the next level of the organization.

Growing up in a middle-class family, where all my relatives had dismissed the opportunity to go to school, along with my grandmother's desire to have a professional in the family, were the driving forces pushing me towards being an accomplished professional. It is now in my blood to have a non-complacency mindset and constantly seek personal growth. *I hope you can relate to this.*

My dreams were being threatened by a group of people who believed they were the rulers of the company and that there was no way a non-experienced kid would change the way they did business. I had all these thoughts racing through my mind and kept circling back to some of the questions I was asked during the job interview and the way I answered them:

The workforce needs to believe the ideas are coming from them!

Eureka! That was the answer I was looking for; now it was up to me to figure out how to make them believe that my ideas were their ideas, or even better, get the improvements or suggestions to come from them. I had to show the company's leadership team the type of manager I was and that the group was performing according to the new objectives set for the department.

After analyzing every member of my team and approaching them individually I began to fit in. This task took quite some time, since I wanted to identify the team members who were the most resistant to change. It was not easy but after spending a great deal of time on the shop floor with them, getting my hands dirty helping them do their jobs, I started to increase my credibility and got to know them both professionally and personally, and they got to know me as well.

I used every conversation to create new ideas and convince them to start doing things a little bit

THE AMERICAN DREAM

differently for their own benefit and the benefit of the company. This was a great learning curve for my career and personal life.

The department itself started to change and perform better, to the extent that some people in other departments wanted to work with us. Monthly department results also showed how our area was exceeding the targets set by the company. My attention was 100% focused on leading people (not managing) and creating results. But it was only a matter of time until I noticed that the area manager was excluding me from company meetings and communication memos. I knew something was wrong but could not figure out what it was. I probably took for granted that everyone in the company welcomed the positive impact we had in the organization.

There is always a person in a team who despite all the efforts you put into something, focuses their existence on negative thinking, envy and disrespect. One day, after discussing with my team members some daily assignments and short-term goals, that individual approached me and asked, in an ironic way, if I had had already found a new job. In my confusion, I asked what he meant. With a big smile on his face, he turned to walk away, mentioning that he had seen a job posting in a local newspaper recruiting for my position.

Andres Gutierrez

The news came as a shock to me, blocking every rational thought I had about the situation. I did not know what to do or how to react. I wanted to run straight to the manager's office and request an explanation, but I had nothing, just the news from this individual. After spending the longest day of my life at work and waiting for my mind to come back to reality, I realized what I needed to do: I had to find the job posting this person was referring to and get answers to my questions.

Feeling a big disappointment and seeing how the foundation of my future as a professional was breaking into pieces, I confirmed that I was living a nightmare – that all this was really happening, and I could not do anything about it.

I learned through a reliable co-worker that I was certainly being replaced. Based on what he said, I figured out that the department manager had teamed up with the individual to bad-talk my performance and discredit all my team's work. I realized that it was too late to change a situation I had not even known I was in, and I discarded any ideas of confronting anyone in the company. Instead, all my thoughts turned into what my family was going to think and how they would react to the news.

THE AMERICAN DREAM

Not long after experiencing the feeling that I had nothing to work towards, I decided to touch base with some friends and find out what they were doing after graduation. My subconscious was probably looking for a way out, a new career path to follow – to my surprise it became a journey to find the people I wanted to talk to. One day I came across a friend from university driving a taxi cab. My conversation with him was long and very shocking. He had never found a decent job opportunity after university. The only job proposal he got offered him no more than the minimum wage. *After listening to the tone of his voice, it sounded like he had already given up.*

He was making a living on the road working 16 hours a day with no breaks or rest; he hardly had the time to see his family. He was living proof of the reality of a country where 60% of the population lived in poverty and the middle class was disappearing, creating a bigger gap between the upper and lower class.

This also showed how a basic economic system works: supply vs. demand. There were so many qualified people looking for jobs that some companies were disrespectfully taking advantage of the situation, compensating workers, even experienced professionals, with something close to the minimum wage.

I learned that most of the people I knew were not around anymore; they had left the country looking for better opportunities abroad. Spain, England, France and the United States were among the preferred destinations. The future was not promising from any point of view; looking for another job and starting all over again was all I had in mind, but I knew that I was going to fall into the same circle of frustration, even if another opportunity would come across.

Unsettled and waiting for the department manager to deliver the news about someone else taking over my area, I began to search the internet for ways to emigrate to any of the countries my friends talked about. Bringing some optimism to my situation, I thought how exciting it would be to see snow and learn another language. This was something I'd often thought of while growing up. My research first focused on the United States, envisioning myself in a country where everyone was living the "American dream."

# Chapter Three

The United States

If we never try, we will never find out. ~Jo Miller

Without further ado I decided to quit my job, and I gave my employer 15 days notice. The area manager could not believe it; I'd never mentioned the fact that I knew about the job posting and the plan they had to replace me. To my surprise, he tried to convince me to stay, stating that my future in the company was very promising. I was not sure what the intention behind those comments was, but at that point I had already made up my mind. I needed to leave and go to a place where I could fulfill all my dreams both personally and professionally.

The thoughts that were motivating me to leave and pursue my dreams elsewhere were also the thoughts that were fighting back, telling me to stay where I was, in my comfort zone. We all go through this process and it is unbelievable how our minds operate with these mixed thoughts and emotions, to the point where we go into a state of limbo. *I know this is a very painful process*. We all need to fight those feelings; overcoming that mental state is one more step on the path to success.

It was not an easy decision to make. I spent long hours thinking about my present situation and many sleepless nights trying to figure out what the future had in store for me. This was the mental torture I went through when I saw the need to leave everything behind in hopes of a better tomorrow. Fearing how our decisions are going to affect us and affect our family are some of the roadblocks that could easily hold us back from moving forward. *Do not let that happen!*

> If you leave room for failure, most likely you are going to fail.

Now it was time to let everyone know of the new plan I had for my future, regardless of what they may think or say. During this stage of the journey, once your mind is made up there should not be a way back, and that thought should always stay fresh in your mind. *If you leave room for failure, most likely you are going to fail.*

The time came when I had to take a leap of faith. All my possessions, the things that I worked so hard for – I had to let them go. Regardless of my next destination, I knew I could not take them with me. My bike, clothing, TV, books, furniture and all the tangible items that made me remember who I was – all my belongings were gone in a fraction of the time it had taken me to acquire them. I am certain that after all these years, relatives, friends of friends and people who I probably do not remember anymore, are still enjoying of something that, at some point, was mine. I still remember the tears coming down my face when I walked away from the building I called home for many years. Letting go of what I had was my first lesson about being attached to physical belongings; realizing that memories, good or bad, are a valuable possession that no one can ever take away from you.

The United States of America was my chosen destination, a country with limitless opportunities and lots of money. What could go wrong? This was it! This was my future.

After finding a place to stay, I needed to figure out how long it would take to learn the language and find a job as a professional. One year was what I had in mind; fortunately, I had some savings that would help me support myself and my family during this transition period.

When I got to the US, I immediately noticed a change: cars everywhere, big and modernized buildings, people always in a hurry, and the fact that everything seemed to be so expensive and fancy compared to what I was used to. All of it was new to me. I spent the first couple of weeks getting to know the system and the city. Of course, you get to know good and bad people. To my good fortune, for the first few months I ended up staying in the living room of good people. During this time, I knew all I had to do was learn the language; this was a no-brainer, I did not have any other option.

As I was not working and needed to make the little money I had last, instead of signing up for a beginner English class I decided to listen to some old cassette-based English courses the guy I was staying with had in his possession. If I was going to spend money on English classes, I knew it would be more beneficial to do it at an advanced level; therefore, learning as much as I could ahead of time would accelerate my proficiency and save me some money for the days to come.

Looking back at those days, something else I did to save money (and I still do to this day) is cut my own hair. My wife finds it funny now, but doing it every time reminds me to remain humble.

For some newcomers, who already know and speak the language, let me tell you that they are already ahead of the game. The transition time for a person who immigrates to North America without any communication skills could be from one to two years. For me, listening to the tapes and watching closed-captioned television shows for kids – mostly *Dora The Explorer* and *Blues Clues* – almost 24/7 was key in getting me to that intermediate or advanced proficiency level I wanted to reach.

After a month had gone by, the time I could stay in the place where I was living was coming to an end. It was a race against the clock. I tried to extend my stay there, but although the people I was staying with were very helpful and patient, reasons beyond their control forced them to limit my time at their place. I needed to find another home to stay in and continue to practice what I learned from the cassettes and television shows. At that point I thought I was making a lot of progress in my communication skills and that I would be able to understand what people were trying to tell me in a daily conversation at a grocery store or coffee shop. In my mind the only area I needed to improve upon was articulating sentences and making myself understood clearly. Later I realized that the progress I had made was minimal.

For the next several months I would end up living in two or three different places. This was not exactly what I had in mind, but I was blessed by having the opportunity to find people willing to help.

As time was passing by, money was running out, as were those willing to offer a helping hand. Despite my communication challenges, I began to apply for jobs in my field of experience and background. I felt excited, as I believed I was ready to move into the next stage of my plan. For two weeks I submitted ten to fifteen job applications per day. I was convinced it was only a matter of time before I was called for an interview; I thought it was that easy.

> Giving up was not part of my formula for success.

THE AMERICAN DREAM

Time passed by and neither a call nor an email was sent back to me, not even to thank me for the application submitted. Frustration and disconcertment started to build up day after day.

Frustration can slow down your progress and get you out of focus – remember to always think about why you left everything behind in the first place.

Suddenly, I remembered something that was said to me by all the people I stayed and spent time with. They assured me that in a foreign country it does not matter what type of professional degree someone may have, if you are an immigrant, the only job opportunities would be in the construction and cleaning service fields. I refused to believe what people were trying to put in my head, fighting the thoughts of how easy it would be to give up. I understood that money and time are your worst enemies during this process, especially when you start to lack these two valuable resources.

Giving up was not part of my formula for success; however, it was very clear to me there was a difference between giving up and seeking opportunities to generate a little bit of income working on any of these jobs. After all, there is nothing wrong with cleaning or construction; in fact, my education was funded by my mom's long hours of hard work cleaning apartments and houses in New York City.

When I started inquiring about opportunities to work in any of these fields, almost everybody I knew was a subject matter expert; they knew all possible connections and people looking for individuals willing to work evenings, midnights and weekends.

It amazed me how knowledgeable everyone was on these topics. Soon, I realized how easy it would be to become consumed by the social environment surrounding me. It is as simple as this: *if you are surrounded by foolish people, you'll become foolish; but if you get close to successful people you will become successful!* Do not forget that it is our choice to choose who we will be surrounded by.

Chapter Four

An American Dream

If you really want something, you will work hard for it. ~Sir Edmund Hillary

My very first employment adventure was in a car wash, and it was quite the experience. It took me almost two hours and three bus transfers to get there from where I was staying. During the commute I felt as if I was sacrificing the valuable time I had to improve my communication skills, just for a long bus ride and a low-paying job that would take me nowhere.

The first time I got to the car wash I had to wait for the owner to show up, even though he knew I would be there. Later that morning I was introduced to the team members, and of course I began to work. The days there were long and exhausting, and although most of the guys I worked with were friendly, I still believe that I got to do most of the work no one wanted to do. *No hard feelings.*

After a few days on the job, I concluded that the commute, low pay and especially the time wasted, was not worth doing all over again the following week and that my first week at the carwash should be the last one. From a money-making standpoint, it did not make sense whatsoever. I was being paid less than the minimum wage and I was only guaranteed four hours of work a day. Believe it or not, I never got paid for my first and only week of work – the carwash owner never showed up on payday. Luckily, I was able to cover the bus fares for my commute with the tips we split up at the end of each work day.

> I decided that I was not going to live the rest of my life doing what was doing.

I decided to give construction a try. As I mentioned before, I had several options, all coming from people that I got to know, or from "a friend of a friend." The hourly wage of one of the opportunities presented to me caught my attention and I went for it. The person I started to work for had gotten a good contract renovating houses. The heavy work explained why the job was well paid; this opportunity was helping me financially, but at the same time it was taking away all the time I had. It became scary when I realized that I was starting to feel comfortable making some money. It was evident I was creating a new comfort zone and that my real objectives were beginning to fade away.

Months were passing by and opportunities to find something in my professional field were more difficult to find. The idea of having the opportunity to practice my communication skills was not happening as frequently as I expected; all the people I worked with spoke my native language. In the little time I had to spare I continued to send my resume to potential job opportunities – entry level, salaried, hourly, contract, employment agencies, you name it. At the end, the outcome of my efforts was already familiar to me: I never got back a single reply.

More time was passing by. I can't deny that my frustration was taking over to the point where I did not know what to do any more. It looked like I did not have any other option but to give up on my dreams and never find the place of endless job opportunities.

During one of my many sleepless nights, I decided that I was not going to live the rest of my life doing what was doing. *What did I go to school for anyway?* This led me to come up with another plan. My new priority was to work harder, save as much money as I could, and then go back home. If I saved enough money, I would probably be able to make a living by buying and managing a couple of taxi cabs for the rest of my life.

During this time, there was a voice at the back of my head shouting very loudly: You are giving up!

    I started to work harder and harder, keeping myself busy trying to ignore and avoid the thoughts of heading back home. Hard work started to pay off; as I was saving some money, I began to invest it in myself. It was time for me to sign up for some English classes late at night. Despite the very few hours of sleep I had in a day, attending the classes was one of best decisions I could have made.

    The classes put everything together for me; all the time spent listening to the tapes, radio talk-shows and watching *Dora the Explorer* had not been a waste after all. In a very short time, most of what I learned started to make sense, and finally I had a group of people helping me and correcting my pronunciation and grammar. I met several individuals in the same situation I was in, having professional degrees, learning the language and strengthening their communication skills to realize their desired American dream.

During one of our many informal conversations, the topic of Canada came up, specifically the weather and job opportunities. No one ever considered moving to Canada as an option, as most of them had already started building a social life where they were. Stepping out of the new comfort zone was very intimidating, especially believing it was too soon to start all over again or not knowing where you would be setting foot.

When I went home, I realized that all I knew about Canada was that it snowed twelve months a year, five days a week and that it was cold all year round. In my mind I pictured penguins wandering down the streets. So I decided to apply one of the business principles I had learned during my university years – it was time to make the current threats into new opportunities. I needed to do some research and find out more about Canada. The perception I had, was probably the perception everyone else had. The internet became my best ally for this task.

> I did not have anything to lose, but there was so much to be won.

During my research, several law and immigration firms appeared on the screen. I had to ignore them all anyway, as I was not going to spend the little money I had on these types of services. I kept looking until I found a government website listing all the provinces, their lifestyles, tourist attractions, economy drivers, main businesses and industries, and even employment opportunities. The websites showed off the beauty of the cities and stated how wonderful it was to live in every single one – it was a healthy competition between provinces and cities to attract people and new talent.

Based on the pictures I saw, all the places looked different, but there was something in common about all of them: they all described how proud they were to be part of Canada. It really amazed me the way Canada and its provinces made themselves so attractive and welcoming to visitors, especially people looking for new opportunities.

From that moment on, my attention was fully focused on Canada. It was not until I looked it up that I learned which languages were spoken. To my surprise and relief, they were English and French; therefore, the time and money spent in the USA learning one of these two languages was not wasted. It was even better when I found out that there were four seasons, but I was a little disappointed when I

THE AMERICAN DREAM

learned that penguins actually live in the Southern Hemisphere.

Here it was, a new door opened wide, waiting for me to go through. All I read about Canada was so exciting and appealing; I did not have anything to lose, but there was so much to be won. All I had to do was use what I had learned during my stay in the USA to recalibrate my plan and finally make my dreams come true. This was a perfect opportunity to show all the family members I left behind that I was an achiever, and finally, make my grandparents proud.

Chapter Five

Canada

Do or do not; there is no try. ~Master Yoda

Once I had my paperwork in order I literally wanted to run to the bus station and head up north; however, all I had left at this point was $110.50 – which was not enough for a bus ticket, food or a night in a motel. I had no choice but to reach out to some of my acquaintances and ask for help – a very uncomfortable situation, as it is not in my nature to go around and ask for money.

I approached the people I was staying with, explaining what I had in mind and telling them all the opportunities ahead of me once I could make it across the border to Canada. The news came as a big surprise to them. Although they expected me to live on my own and settle down in the city, they did not want me to leave and start all over again without knowing anything else about this new country.

I remembered when I'd sat down with my own family and explained why I wanted to come to North America in the first place; it was a very similar situation with my friends. Even though their arguments were valid and I understood the point they wanted to make, I knew this time everything was going to be different. Unfortunately, there was not an easy way to articulate in words all the faith I had in this opportunity.

I did not ask for any money. The only help I asked for was getting the bus tickets, and I did not want to take anything else from them. Without hesitation they helped me with my request. I took the money as a loan and planned to pay it back. They stated, however, that they did not want the money back.

The bus trip I was considering taking was a one-way ride to a small town right on the American and Canadian border. Once there, I planned to take a taxi cab to the Canadian customs office on the other side of the bridge. After spending long hours on the bus fighting all the fears of the unknown, a sense of calmness started to flow through my body once I saw what appeared to be a big river dividing two great nations.

Upon my arrival at the bus station I approached several cab drivers to explain my situation. Their response was something I had not planned on: due to immigration issues and border protection laws, they would not go across the border. I remember thinking that the only way to overcome this small obstacle and make it to the other side of the bridge was to walk. To this day, I still find it very funny and unforgettable … there could never be a more interesting way to set foot in a new country.

I✼I

It took almost 30 minutes to make it to the other side of the bridge. It felt as if I was walking for hours on a walkway that had no end. During that time, there were so many thoughts and flashbacks raising so many questions concerning the integrity of my journey; some of those thoughts challenged simple facts as to why I

> The welcome sign made me feel home again regardless of the uncertainty of my future.

THE AMERICAN DREAM

was there in that very moment or why I left home in the first place. As all these thoughts started to come up, my body experienced all kinds of unrecognizable feelings, to the point where it appeared that the doubts were taking over my dreams.

As I walked on, the bridge seemed to be growing in length. Entire families driving by were looking at me in surprise and wondering what I was doing. Every time that happened, I just looked away and let myself get lost in the storm of thoughts going through my head. I do not think very many people cross that border by foot, so I guess my actions were providing some sort of entertainment to families and drivers in their commute to their different destinations.

I remember trying to look ahead, struggling to find the end of the bridge. It was a walk without an end. All I was able to see was the arch created by the structure of the bridge in the middle of it. To my comfort, a sign started to appear very slowly at the far end of the bridge. It felt like a miracle when I read: Welcome to Canada! The Canadian flag was clearly visible next to it, waving along with the wind. My eyes watered in seconds, and all my doubts and fears disappeared instantly. The welcome sign made me feel home again regardless of the uncertainty of my future and having no idea where I would spend the night or what I would be having for dinner that day.

When I set foot in Canada, everything seemed so different – for some reason the air, the streets, the people, everything looked so different and perfect. I am glad that was my very first impression of the country that I now proudly call home.

When I made it to the immigration booth, presented my documentation and explained my situation to the Canadian Border Services officer with the very limited communication skills I had, I was advised to go to an office at the other side of the building and wait for another officer to help me. It did not take very long for help to come my way and for me to realize that I was right about how friendly Canadians are.

After going through some paperwork and verifying my identity, they gave me a list of potential cities in the province and all their available shelter locations where assistance was offered to individuals in my situation. I thought I was misunderstanding what I was being told. The officer had to repeat several times what he was telling me. I could not believe how, in just matter of hours, some of my worries were taken care of by a country and people that knew very little or nothing about me.

THE AMERICAN DREAM

Since I was not expecting what was happening, it took me a while to consider the options on the list of shelters they'd given me and to make up my mind as to where I was supposed to go. The only logical option, with the very little information I had, was the capital of the province, the biggest city. Even though there would be more competition in the job market and the chances to succeed faster in a small city would be greater, my priority was to get to know the system and continue to learn the language. *Work was a priority as well, that's why I was there in the first place, but I needed to walk before being able to run.*

After I told the officer where I wanted to go, and with only $55 left in my pockets, they made all the necessary arrangements for my two-hour car ride to the city – it was unbelievable how well everything was working out. When I made it to the shelter, there was a young woman already waiting for me to arrive. She checked me in, advising me that in the morning I would have an orientation session where the rules of the place would be explained to me and finalizing our conversation by walking with me to my room. That night I fell asleep very quickly, relieving my mind and my body of the thoughts and the anxieties I'd experienced those days.

Chapter Six

A Professional Path

For out in this world we find/ Success begins with a fellow's will/ It's all in the state of mind. ~Walter D. Wintle

There was a knock on the door the next morning, waking me up instantly. When I answered, a female voice advised that the cafeteria was serving breakfast until just 10:00 a.m. and she would be waiting for me in the main office once I was finished.

After having a bowl of cereal and some fruit, I headed to the office to meet with her. She was waiting for me with a folder and lots of information, ready to answer any questions I might have. My first questions focused on how to get some assistance to improve my communication skills and finding out any ways to validate my professional studies. She took some notes, highlighting some of my background and my professional expertise. Very kindly, she advised me that someone would be getting back to me with all the requirements needed to validate my university credentials, but right away she handed me a list of institutions that provided educational, social and employment services to newcomers to the city. I could not have been more excited about these new opportunities and the circumstances surrounding me – there was certainly a light at the end of the tunnel.

On my way out the main office, I saw several picture frames with the names and photos of the volunteers at the shelter. Most of them were university students trying to assist others in any way they could, the social worker explained. I was impressed when I learned that they did not charge any money or expect anything in return when working at the shelter.

That day I learned the true meaning of volunteering – this concept intrigued me to the point that I wanted to do the same. In fact, as it was explained to me later on, this was one of the rules and expectations of the shelter for someone to be able to stay. With some help from the students, I needed to find a volunteering opportunity in a public institution, non-profit organization, or anywhere in the city, where I might be able to help others in my spare time, without expecting any remuneration in return. I learned a very valuable skill no university in the world would be able to teach me: the sense of people caring for each other and being able to do something meaningful just for the sake of being true to ourselves, and money was not part of the equation.

During this stage of my journey I was trying to learn how the system operated. Luckily everything was working to my advantage. I was being given the opportunity to go to school, interact with others and, at the same time, pay back all that was given to me through volunteering. I could not believe how fortunate I was, and I did not know who to thank but the system and the people around me.

Later that day I came across some of the volunteers at the shelter. They all knew who I was, and this made it easy to start a conversation with them. During our first discussions, one of the volunteers offered to take me to have my English assessed and sign up for a proper class. As the conversation continued, I realized that the more questions they asked about me and my plans for the future, the more anxious I was becoming to make myself understood fluently. It was the first time I had the opportunity to establish a real and long conversation with English-speaking people.

THE AMERICAN DREAM

Fortunately for me, while I was talking to them, they were correcting my pronunciation and my grammar. This encouraged me to try harder without worrying about making a mistake or being made fun of because of my accent or vocabulary limitations. Having great people assisting me one-on-one was making a big difference to my progress. The more I tried to express myself without any hesitations, the more I realized that focusing on my communication skills would be a stepping stone in my adaptation to the system.

We looked at the list of institutions and selected four or five; they were located mostly within the same area, making it easy for us to visit them in one or two days. The trips would also help me to get to know the city, and most importantly, the public transit system.

During my subway and bus trips, I saw many people reading the newspaper, listening to music or just chatting with friends. They all seemed to be focused on what they were doing, but at the same time so comfortable in the life they were living. It was a feeling I had not experienced for a long time. I even pictured myself in the future, commuting to my workplace, all settled down. Within only couple days in the country, I knew I had made the right choice to come to Canada.

At the first school, I noticed quite a few people completing their assessment test. I got a little nervous, since this test was going to tell me how far I would be from being fluent in my communication. During the test, my grammar and reading skills were challenged, but the real test, in my opinion, was when they assessed my listening and comprehension skills – they played a tape and asked me to answer several simple questions. When I was listing to the tape to complete my final evaluation, I thought everything I was listening to was making sense – I thought it was an easy test. However, when the instructor evaluated my answers, I learned that I was hardly making it into an intermediate level.

> My desire to succeed made me capable of doing what was necessary to achieve my goals.

After the assessment was done, I realized that it would be over a year before I felt comfortable enough to start applying for jobs in my professional field without being rejected or having my application ignored due to communication limitations.

When it comes to finding an employment opportunity, or the right opportunity – I must say, the timeline factor was critical for two main reasons: the

THE AMERICAN DREAM

first one was the fact that I had not been employed all this time, creating a misperception of "laziness." The second reason was around the time-gap between jobs – this could have also created an impression of lack of continuous work experience. After several interview sessions, I understood how important it was to articulate very well why the gap between jobs was there.

Once we had visited all the schools and were headed back to the shelter, I had a sense of what my life would be like for the next year or two. I had to fine-tune my plan and focus on what I needed to do first. I looked at the programs and schedules the institutions offered, and I decided to enroll in two different courses: one was a full-time class from 9:00 a.m. to 3:30 p.m., and the other was a part-time option, from 6:00 p.m. to 9:30 p.m. Some of the volunteers at the shelter thought it would be too much to handle – including the time I would be volunteering – but I knew I had to try. From the bottom of my heart, I knew I would be able to do it. *My desire to succeed made me capable of doing what was necessary to achieve my goals.*

In the full-time program, I was lucky to be in a course with only eight other students. This gave me more access to the tutor, to ask as many questions as necessary and be corrected when I needed to be corrected. This was the perfect setting to increase my vocabulary and improve my speaking skills. The second program was more crowded, as most of the people attending this course were coming after work. In this course the grammar was more intense, improving my writing and reading skills. Let me tell you that these two courses were the perfect combination to accelerate my progress and fluency.

I met interesting people in both courses, but they all had something in common – they came to Canada looking for better opportunities and a better future for themselves and their families. They came from Europe, Asia, Africa, Central and South America. It was a perfect mix of cultures, backgrounds and dreams.

There were also three people with professional degrees and lots experience in their fields – one of them was a doctor, one a lawyer, and the third was a computer engineer. The doctor and the lawyer had a long way to go if they wanted to work in their fields of experience, as the requirements to validate their studies and professional degrees were more complex than mine. The computer guy once came to me and asked what my plan was to work in my field. I had it clear, my plan was to become fluent and then apply for jobs. He said something very interesting that

THE AMERICAN DREAM

certainly changed the game plan – this is the power of networking.

He mentioned that there were some non-profit organizations assisting foreign-trained professionals to have a smooth transition into the Canadian system, increasing the opportunities to interact with different companies and mentors, at the same time creating more chances to find a job suitable for our professions. He provided me with the names of two institutions and told that he had an appointment with a counselor the very next day.

When I made it back to the shelter that day, and even before I had the opportunity to complete some research, one of the volunteers was waiting for me at the lounge area with good news for me. It was time to go out and look for a place of my own, where I could have some independence and continue with my transition into the Canadian system. *This opportunity was also one of the privileges offered by the system to individuals who wanted to follow the rules and truly contribute to society in the long term.*

After a month or so searching for a place, we found a small comfortable apartment on the top floor of a five-story building; the view of the houses surrounding the area was great. It was the perfect spot to start a life. I guess it was easy for me to move in as

I just had a suitcase with my clothes; however, and to my surprise – one more time – I was also given an appointment at a furniture bank. Hearing the term for the first time, it was explained to me that I just needed to go there, take a look at the items they had in their warehouse and select what I thought I needed for my new place. What can I say? It was a blessing to have the opportunity to be in Canada and to meet helpful people who expected nothing in return.

When I checked the information provided by the computer guy on the foreign-trained professional support organization, I found links for more non-profit institutions offering courses in multiple disciplines and subjects. All these had one simple objective: to strengthen an individual's education and background. There was so much information to look at, but so little time. I immediately called and booked an appointment with one of the counselors for the following week. I recall having a smile on my face when I realized that it was the same appointment the computer guy was attending when I last talked to him. Unfortunately, he

> I did not feel as if I was trying to achieve a crazy dream or a life that did not exist.

had to move to a different area in the city and I lost track of him – I never learned how his journey went.

The following week, when I attended the appointment at the agency, I realized that it was not only an office building with counselors, but more of a research centre with a great deal of information for professionals and individuals looking for help. While I waited for my meeting, I looked around and analyzed my surroundings, seeing very attentive people assisting individuals with all sorts of questions and unclear paths to follow. In this place I saw people like me following the same dreams and objectives; somehow, I did not feel as if I was trying to achieve a crazy dream or a life that did not exist.

My counselor was a very helpful woman, with lots of knowledge and experience assisting people in my situation. For the first time, I did not need to express myself in much detail for someone to understand what I was going through and what I needed to do. I spent almost an hour with her, and at the end of the session, I had a full plan with all the steps I needed to follow to find a job opportunity in my field. The only thing, once again, was that I needed to further improve my language skills – she acknowledged that and so did I. On a positive note, right after my conversation with her, I noticed that the more exposure I had to different people and multiple conversation scenarios, the more comfortable and fluent I was becoming – *hooray!!!*

For those of you who may feel frustrated learning a new skill or who believe you are not making progress towards your objective, I can only say that if you are doing what's right, you must convince yourself that it is unavoidable not to achieve your goal. That thought should encourage you to keep your head up looking forward to the future.

Chapter Seven

The Plan

You've got to be sure of yourself before you can ever win a prize. ~Napoleon Hill

Although I'd always known what I needed to do, I finally had a concrete career transition plan and a path to follow. It was clear to me that I needed to continue to attend the classes I'd signed up for, as well as take advantage of some strategic courses that were offered by the other government/non-profit institutions we found. These courses were designed to assist foreign-trained professionals by teaching them how to create strong resumes and/or get updated on new technical knowledge and local regulations. My hope was that my background, coupled with these specialty courses, would get me to the same level as someone with studies and degrees from Canadian universities.

While attending both the full-time and part-time English courses during the week, I also decided to enroll in a Saturday morning resume and interview preparation class. The counselor recommended this class and thought it was a good idea to prepare myself for future interviews.

The course worked in my favor in two different ways: The first one was the fact that I was familiarizing myself with the North American, and mostly, Canadian style of resume preparation and presentation. Here, I understood that companies were more focused on work experience and not education. I learned the value of the so called "Canadian Experience" concept – which for most employers is worth a lot more than the highest marks from a college, or even, a degree with honors from a well-known university anywhere in the world. The second advantage of taking this class was that I was able to intensively practice my communication skills and interact with more people. *This part was priceless.*

After my first six months of preparation and hard work, I noticed that the intensity and desire of learning made my proficiency in my communication skills much better than expected. I quickly moved into a higher proficiency level and, without realizing it, I was successfully completing essays, delivering presentations, and having long and enjoyable conversations with all the people I encountered daily.

At this point, I was ready to start courses in business topics, and finally, reflect on my resume my interest in education and continuous learning. I was proud of myself and very impressed with the progress I'd made in such a short time.

You must remain humble, but there is nothing wrong with patting yourself on the back from time to time.

After I completed the due diligence and found courses related to my education and work experience, I slowly began to disengage myself from the part-time classes I was attending in the evenings, switching the priorities to business-oriented courses. I had no time to waste.

> I needed to keep on following my plan.

All these events and activities surrounding my life were giving me the opportunity to execute my master plan; getting me ready to find a part-time job to support myself financially. Although it was not the right time to seek an employment opportunity in my field yet, I slowly started to look at the job market by peeking at postings, so I could get a better sense of the expectations and basic requirements a company would look for in a candidate like me.

During my search I found the term "Canadian Experience" all over the job ads, pretty much putting aside educational expectations and asking potential candidates to have at least one year of experience before applying, even for entry level positions. I knew I could not expect to become a business executive right away, but at this point, I was not worried about it – I needed to keep on following my plan.

My routine for the next few months was attending the business courses and going to school in the mornings. On one of those days an acquaintance mentioned that if I was interested, he knew someone who could offer me a cleaning job in a banquet hall; one of his buddies could even offer me a part-time job working with him in his snow plowing business. The financial necessity I was in forced me not to resist any of these offers. The good news

> I knew I could not let those feelings win the battle, but they seemed to have more ammunition and power than before.

THE AMERICAN DREAM

though, was that none of these was affecting my plan in any way.

After I completed the courses, had my resume up to date and was somewhat familiar with the system, I decided to start applying for jobs in my field. I was convinced that it was a matter of weeks or probably couple months, at the most, before I would start working for a big corporation. There were several job postings popping up in my daily search that I thought I would be a good match for. I committed myself to sending as many applications as possible per day, hoping for the telephone to ring for that so-desired interview opportunity.

It was not until several months down the road after not getting a single reply to my applications, I realized that something was still missing from my plan. The feelings and frustrations I experienced at that moment were taking over my desire for success, making the negative thoughts from the past appear one more time. I knew I could not let those feelings win the battle, but they seemed to have more ammunition and power than before.

During my part-time job experience and time passing by, I made some friends and started to build a comfortable social life. I met people with different goals and objectives, and everyone I came across fit into two different categories:

> In the first category were the ones that I call the "homesick." They just wanted to work eighteen hours a day, seven days a week, make as much money as possible and then go back to their home country and live off the money they had saved. *I remember that at some point I fell into this category.*
>
> In the second category, the "go-with-the flow" kind of people, you can find individuals who like to live a quiet life and survive by just making the minimum wage; taking one day at the time without worrying about the future, but with no future.
>
> *Something was clear to me: no matter how far away I was from my dream, I could not let myself fall into either of these two categories.*

Keeping in mind the circumstances I was living in, I tried to picture myself in one of these two categories. I found that as for the first one, it was too late for me. Canada had already started to invade my mind and soul, and I could not see myself going back to where I came from. Regardless of my current situation, I was in love with the country and its

THE AMERICAN DREAM

people. As for the second category, I realized that I was already living that life, but I was missing the happy part in it. I was not pleased with my professional accomplishments thus far, as there were not any.

At one of those social events that were part of my new life style, I remember attending a barbeque (one of the many passions for Canadians) when one of my friends introduced me to his father, who had moved to the country almost twenty-five years ago, and through hard work and dedication built a successful painting business. His company had a very large client base with lucrative contracts with well-known property management firms in the city – he seemed to be in a good financial situation.

During our conversation, we discussed stuff everyone talks about at a social event: the weather, sports, the economy, family and so on. At a certain stage in the conversation, when he felt somewhat comfortable with me, he asked about my professional experience and wanted to know if I was working in something related to my background.

The questions were surprising until I realized that my friend had probably told him that I had a professional degree and was constantly searching for employment opportunities in my area of experience. I explained what I was doing and told him what my plans were. I thought that a person with the track record of success he had was about to offer me valuable advice – words of encouragement to once again fuel my desire for success and bring back the non-complacency mentality I had when I had first arrived to the country.

I was not expecting to hear what he did say to me. His words were like darts coming out of his mouth. Those words – from where I stand today – served as a wake-up call that fulfilled the encouragement I was hungry for.

> *Do not waste your time doing what you're doing. You have to find a full-time job in whatever is offered to you and move on. I know lots of people like you, people with professional degrees that after so much time wasted, came to me looking for employment. I now have accountants, engineers, lawyers, and so forth working for me painting apartments, basements, you name it ... and let me tell you that they are very happy now.*

Even though these words were not new to me, my head started to spin around, and my throat felt clogged – I could not even swallow. After listening to him, I was not able to articulate a single sentence. His painful piece of advice was what I needed to put myself back on track and stimulate my thoughts to find a proper solution to my situation. *One more person to prove wrong.*

Chapter Eight

A New Door Opens

Discipline, trust and perseverance – it's also an answer to many people's questions. ~AG

There was only one place that had the knowledge and the expertise to help me get out of the social cycle and mentality I'd gotten myself into. The agency assisting foreign-trained professionals had the answers I was starving for; for some strange reason I had not taken full advantage of all the assistance they offered me in the first place and did not leverage the human resources connections, talent and experience they had to help me.

I called my counselor trying to arrange for an appointment. During our short telephone conversation, she expressed her concerns that I hadn't come back to our follow-up sessions. This could have created a negative perception of my professionalism as it might have reflected some lack of interest on my part in the services they offered. Nevertheless, she was very happy to hear back from me and was very impressed with the progress I'd made with my communication skills, acknowledging how well-spoken I'd become.

Shortly after I met with her in person, she updated all my records in the system and was very happy to know that during this time I'd completed some career focused and technical courses to strengthen my educational background. She advised me that from an educational perspective, I had an advantage compared to the other foreign-trained professionals she had worked with in the past. I explained to her that I was constantly applying for jobs but never got any feedback from prospective employers. She was not surprised to know that I had received no replies from any of my employment applications.

Once again, I heard the term "Canadian Experience" coming from her, and certainly there was no mention of it in my resume or cover letter. The first big dilemma, as she explained to me, was that it is important to have a strong educational background, but experience is key when it comes to companies deciding who they want to hire, especially for those coming from other countries. As we live in a multicultural country, in some people's minds the different cultural, religious, and social backgrounds may create a conflict in the workplace. As a safeguard, they want to hire people who have already been exposed to it in a workplace environment.

Now, the second biggest dilemma, which is very difficult for corporations to understand, is this:

> *If no one offers an employment opportunity to a professional, no matter where he or she comes from or who they are – doctors, lawyers, engineers, and so on – how can anyone get the so-called Canadian Experience needed to be part of the Canadian workforce?*

This is a reality faced not only by foreign-trained professionals looking for employment in a new country, but also for recent Canadian university graduates. The Canadian system has recognized that this is a common problem, and in order to solve it they have created different programs to facilitate this transition, helping us work and partner with other non-profit organizations and different corporations to facilitate this process.

THE AMERICAN DREAM

When I heard these words, a big smile was drawn on my face, realizing that she had something in mind for me to do. I was very anxious to hear what it was but did not want to interrupt her while she was explaining the whole situation to me.

She asked me if I was interested in a mentorship program, as she felt I was ready for it. At that point I had decent communication skills, good education, exposure to the Canadian educational system, and most importantly, the desire and commitment to be successful. Not knowing exactly what the program was, my answer was *YES!* I trusted what she was offering me and, of course, the system itself. During her explanation, she stated that in this program I would be matched up with an experienced Canadian professional working in the same field I had experience in. She also said that the mentor, after an initial face-to-face interview and three more in the field sessions, could offer me an employment opportunity through the company he or she was working for in partnership with the non-profit government agency.

> I felt like an Olympic athlete looking at the countdown clock ready to start a race.

Andres Gutierrez

I wanted to give her a big hug as I realized this was a big breakthrough and the only chance I had to fairly compete for a job opportunity in my field. Unfortunately, the program did not have enough mentors for the number of professionals looking for opportunities. Since the mentorship program was managed by a partner agency, I needed to submit my application with all my personal information, including university transcripts and previous work experience, through an online recruitment process. It turned out that due to the high demand, they were only accepting applications late at night in three different online sessions lasting from five to fifteen minutes. The application process was taking place from 1:00 to 3:00 a.m. on three different weekdays.

I got all the information I needed from my counselor: website, personal code, enrollment dates, etc. I had all I needed to apply for one of the opportunities offered. The first night I was very anxious and patiently waiting for the time to come.

When the session opened, I started filling out the application very carefully, making sure every single field and question was completed to the best of my knowledge and ability, without realizing time was running faster than usual. When I finished and hit the "submit" icon on the computer screen, it was too late for the system to accept my application and it kicked me out of the session right away. For a second, I got a little worried but told myself that at least I had two more chances to try.

The following day, once again, I was anxiously waiting for the session to start. I was biting my nails and looking at the clock on the computer for the exact start time to come – I felt like an Olympic athlete looking at the countdown clock ready to start a race.

When the session began, knowing ahead of time the questions I needed to answer, I completed the application faster than the previous day. However, after I submitted my application several times, the system very quickly generated a message advising that there were many applications being processed and I needed to submit mine once again or try another day.

I was becoming more and more anxious and frustrated about the process, creating some skepticism – I started to believe that I was going to miss this great opportunity.

Once again, the online session expired without my application going through. I could not sleep for the rest of the night thinking of getting hold of my counselor to ask if this was a normal situation in the process. When I did, she told me not to worry and suggested that I needed to do it one more time during the next and last available session, which was scheduled for the following day. Otherwise, I would have to wait until summertime when the next mentorship program started. She could not do anything else from her end, but she gave me something very valuable: her support and advice. I had one more shot and was determined to take full advantage of it.

The rest of the day was very long, and the time passed by very slowly. My anxiety did not help me at all; my mind was focused and prepared for the last application session to start all over again.

When the time came closer for the application process to begin, I sat patiently in front of the computer and waited for the webpage to load. Once again, I quickly and accurately completed the application form, right before hitting the submit button. Once again, I got the same message telling me that the system was busy processing the application and asking me to try again in couple minutes.

I remembered I had no other option but to keep trying during the ten minutes I had left for the last session to be done. After nine minutes trying without success, I relentlessly continued to hit submit

… submit … submit … for the last minute I had left, getting the same message back: *System is busy, try again later! System is busy, try again later! System is busy, try again later!* I lost the sense of time in that last remaining minute. However, on my very last try, a new message popped up on the screen, showing me something I had not seen before. The message provided me with a registration number and advised I would be contacted soon by a member of their staff.

Chapter Nine

Mentorship

A lot of people have gone further than they thought they could because someone else thought they could.
~Zig Ziglar

With lots of excitement I contacted my counselor to deliver the great news: *I had made it into the program!* She also felt very pleased that I was able to have my application processed in the system. She told me it would work to my advantage that I had already completed some resume and interview preparation courses in the past. These courses were the ones offered by the non-profit organizations I engaged with in the early stages of the transition to my new country.

The mentorship program was structured in such a way that the members needed to take these courses as part of the curriculum foundation. Now, being ahead of the game, I would quickly start meeting with my potential mentor(s).

Within a week or so I got a phone call from the program coordinator asking me to participate in an information session in which the program benefits, rules and expectations from all parties involved – the mentorship organization, the mentors and mentees – would be explained.

In the information session there were approximately 20 of us, full of excitement, energy and looking as if we had already landed a great job opportunity. In reality, just being part of the program was already a big accomplishment. For all of us, this was the closest we had made it into the job market, a real corporation, and possibly real employment.

While the host of the session explained to us how the program worked and the economics around wages and benefits, we were given a personalized envelope with the background information on our matched mentors and the meeting dates where we would finally get to opportunity to meet them. She requested to us not to open the envelope right away, but rather wait until the following session. She also advised that in the envelope we would find our mentor's name, their job title, the industry of the company they were part of, and so forth. In a separate session, these very same instructions were given to the mentors.

Andres Gutierrez

The fact that the Canadian government was subsidizing part of our wages and offering other grants to the participating employers opened the door for individuals with professional degrees and zero Canadian experience the ability to work for a Canadian company, and to finally gain the so-desired Canadian Experience. We could therefore become competitive in the job market and follow a career path related to our area of experience.

The second orientation session of the program was scheduled for the following week. This was the session where we would all be meeting the individuals willing to help us. During that session, while I excitedly waited for the facilitator and mentor to approach me, I reviewed the paperwork provided to me with my mentor's information and company profile. When I pulled the information out of the envelope, I confirmed at a glance, that he was a very experienced manager whose career was focused in different industries. He had worked in several countries around the world and finally settled in Canada 15 years ago.

The good news was that his area of expertise was the same as mine (the mentorship program certainly made sure of that). I had waited approximately five minutes when I noticed the session's facilitator waiving her hand at me indicating

THE AMERICAN DREAM

to come and see her. To my surprise she was by herself and explained that my mentor could not make it to the session. She also said that he would schedule a meeting with me later at his office.

That day, with additional time on my hands, I went in detail through my mentor's profile and professional information, learning that his cultural background was not Canadian at all. I could not even pronounce his last name. He had actually lived and knew very well the newcomer transition process, the very same process I was going through. He had decided to help professionals in the same circumstances he was in when he first came to the country.

> I had limited time and needed to take advantage of every single opportunity given to me.

The day came when I had the opportunity to meet with him, and during our first conversation I discovered he was a very knowledgeable person, willing to help. Most importantly, he had lots of experience in my field and knew the industry very well. I noticed a little bit of disappointment from his end when he realized that I was not from the same geographical location where he originally came from.

I assumed that he was probably expecting someone from the same country of origin as himself.

During our dialogue, I came to the conclusion that the nationality, religion, and cultural background mismatch were not going to affect our relationship. Nevertheless, I suspected I might not be getting all the attention I needed (or wanted) and expected from him at that point. I knew I had limited time and needed to take advantage of every single opportunity given to me and, of course, pay attention to all advice coming from him.

Our first meeting must have gone well; that very same day I was asked to meet with the company's human resources department, where I was presented with what would be my very first contract with a Canadian company. After completing all the required paperwork and agreeing to follow the organization's code of conduct and policies, I was, somewhat, an employed professional.

The offer letter showed the total number of hours that I was expected to work per week and the hourly rate I would receive in compensation; fifty percent of it was covered by the mentorship program (or Canadian government). The document also revealed that I would be getting only the minimum provincial wage.

THE AMERICAN DREAM

I was so blown away by the opportunity of being accepted into the program that I had never paid attention to how much the pay would be; and when I thought about it later in the process, I was hesitant to ask as I did not want to disappoint anyone and potentially giving the wrong impression to the staff managing the mentorship program. I wanted them to know that I all cared about was the chance given to me, not the compensation. All I had in my mind was that I was one step closer to making my dreams come true.

It was a great experience when I first started in the company; I got to know the team and the work environment. It was a nice feeling – very different compared to my previous work experiences. Of course, there were people from different backgrounds, ages and nationalities. They were willing to help and assist whenever I needed it. To my surprise, in the team I was now part of, there was a guy from the same country I was born in; he was very friendly and cooperative as well.

During the first couple of weeks I got to know the internal processes and the company's operations, my interaction with my mentor – the area manager – was minimal, but at that time I was not worried about it, since I was busy working and interacting with my new team.

Andres Gutierrez

At the beginning I wanted to focus on the individual from my country of origin, who had been with the organization for approximately five years. I wanted to know all his experiences in the workplace as a professional and as an established Canadian employee. He had a technical degree from his homeland, but after arriving in Canada, his main focus had been to complete a two-year certification program with a recognized college before trying to explore or apply for roles of increased responsibility. He believed he would not have a chance to climb the corporate ladder if he did not have a certificate or some sort of university diploma.

During the few times I had the chance to meet with my mentor, I noticed that our conversations were very short and to the point; he always seemed to be in a hurry and acted as if he did not have anything to share with me at all. This behavior, or lack of time I should say, was jeopardizing the purpose of the mentorship program.

I was there starving for advice for my professional development and future career opportunities, but our conversations would always go around the questions I had about the company and my daily work assignments.

THE AMERICAN DREAM

It would be fair to say that I was not exactly sure what to ask or say; however, I always started our conversation by discussing the tasks I was performing. I did not receive any feedback on the skills that I needed to develop or what technical concepts I needed to improve to become a better professional and excel within my group.

> I am still very thankful for the opportunity and time given to me.

I still remember the way he used to finish the answers to all my questions. It was always:

What else? What else? What else?

It did not matter if it was a technical question or a career-focused one; every time we met our conversation would go like this:

Me: What would be the best way to reach out to potential employers after the mentorship program is finished?

Mentor: You need to have a good resume with lots of Canadian experience and you probably need to complete a certification at a college or university. What else?

Andres Gutierrez

Me: How did you make it into a managerial position in Canada? What would be your recommendation for someone new to the job market?

Mentor: Well, I had connections and you just need to meet your employer's expectations, so you have a secure job. What else?

The *what else?* question at the end of each answer was somewhat uncomfortable and annoying. I guess there was nothing wrong with that, but I needed and wanted to know more, especially if he had any plans for me after the mentorship program was finished. The *what else?* question, or to be more specific, the *what else?* answer, was something that I wanted to avoid every time an answer was given. Don't get me wrong, I am still very thankful for the opportunity and time given to me.

I came to realize that the only hope I had to learn anything new was from the individual who came from the same country I did. His advice was not much different from what I had heard before: *immigrants do not have the same job opportunities as people who studied and graduated from a Canadian university*. I did not see in him any passion or desire for professional growth; it seemed that all he cared about was having job security – *there's nothing wrong with that, of course.*

After a couple of months, I learned how to balance my limited income, and even though it was not very much I managed to improve my lifestyle a bit. The minimum wage got me into a better financial situation than before. *I cannot tell you how grateful I am for the food banks in the area where I lived.*

Since I was not sure if I was going to stay with the corporation once the mentorship program was finished, the next challenge I had in mind was to find an employment opportunity where I could follow a path similar to the one followed by the guy working for this company – the constant "there're no opportunities for foreigners" feedback made me visualize myself doing something like him and living a decent life.

The mentorship program was supposed to last no more than six months, but after the third month there, I realized that I had some of the necessary Canadian Experience under my belt. One day, I saw an internal job posting for an engineering position in a different department – the job requirements also matched my education and previous experience. With some excitement I showed my friend the internal posting. He did not look surprised at all, replying back to me: Oh, yes, I saw it the other day! I asked him why he did not mention it before. His answer took me to a different level of understanding as to why some people do not succeed. He did not have any drive for success nor intentions of growing professionally, or even personally.

He said to me:

> *Don't even bother applying for that job – neither you nor I fit in. That department hires a different type of people.*

I was shocked after listening to his statement. I immediately needed to talk to my mentor and get his input, but it took a couple days before I had the chance to meet with him. His thoughts about the job posting, and the fact that it was a perfect match for me, were no different from my friend's; however, he kind of opened a new door for me. He told me that I was doing a great job and that he was considering extending the mentorship program for three more months and that if everything went well, three more months after that. This got me a bit excited, but the downside was, same pay rate and no benefits. Just the fact of having a potential extension to my stay in the company was something great after all, *wasn't it?*

THE AMERICAN DREAM

I reflected for a couple of days over what to do next. Having the opportunity to be there for three or six more months was an option, but there was a second one: updating my resume and applying for other jobs. After all, I now had some of that Canadian Experience some potential employers refer to.

Chapter Ten

Why be complacent?

We shall have no better conditions in the future if we are satisfied with all these which we have at present.
~Thomas Edison

It did not take much to have my resume updated, and I even had a good conversation with my friend in the company as I needed to have a professional reference ready in case I was called back for an interview. His position was not very encouraging, but supportive. His belief was that the economy and the job market were very slow, and no one was hiring at that moment.

A positive mind looks at every situation from different perspectives. My position was clear: regardless of the state of the economy, there is always someone looking for great people willing to do a remarkable job, and the good news was that that someone was me. I just needed to apply for the right job, in the right company, at the right time. It was like the saying: *Great things come from being in the right place at the right time.*

Within weeks, I received two replies, one from a company looking to arrange a pre-screening phone interview, and another from a different company asking for a date and time for a face-to-face interview. I could not believe it when I realized that two different organizations were interested in my services. I knew I was not going to be a manager or the head of a big department, but an entry level position was all I needed to start with.

I followed some of the tips I'd learned from my previous interview and resume preparation courses – I wrote down all the possible questions and my answers for the pre-screening interview. I prepared myself so much for that phone call that there was no way I was going to fail. I even arranged for the phone interview to happen before I had the opportunity to meet face-to-face with the HR manager for the second job interview. If anything were to go wrong with the

> A positive mind looks at every situation from different perspectives.

pre-screening questions or answers during the phone call, it would work as a lesson learned for the next one.

When the phone rang, I was so nervous that I crumpled my notes by holding the paper so hard. It took me couple seconds to compose my thoughts before picking up the receiver. The first questions, of course, were kind of easy. I introduced myself and asked some friendly questions. The challenging part happened when the technical questions were asked. I was so focused on the notes I had in my hand and tried to read what I had on them that I could not answer the way I wanted. After the call ended, I was afraid I had missed the only chance I had to move into the next stages of the recruiting process; I should have been myself and answered the questions to the best of my ability. On the positive side, it was a good experience and knew that I could do better on the next one.

For the second interview, I needed to look professional somehow, and I remember that I had to unpack my graduation suit, which was now several years old. The only problem was that the coat sleeves and the pants were too short – but I came up with a solution: I would take off the coat as soon I entered the interview room. As for the short pants, the only thing I could do was get as close as possible to a desk so no one would be able to notice that little detail – sure enough that was exactly what I did.

All I had in my mind was to smile the entire time and leave a great first impression. The interview session went quite well. I overcame my nervousness by thinking that I had nothing to lose, I made sure I was myself and answered the questions in such a way that they all addressed exactly what the hiring manager wanted to hear. That day I did something that took me several years to realize:

> *A successful interview happens when the job seeker tells a compelling story that the interviewer can relate to, and it is key to reiterate what he or she wants to hear.* <u>*We need to become storytellers*</u>*.*

The only way to achieve this is by having a conversation and forgetting that you are in an actual job interview. You need to ask as many questions as possible – good, smart questions – so you can figure out what the person you are talking to really wants.

Sure enough, a week later I got a phone call from the head of the human resources department of the company I had the face-to-face interview with. She said that they would like to make me an offer and needed to know a potential start date. I got so excited that I remained quiet on the phone to the point where she knew I did not know how to answer the unexpected questions. After a short giggle, she advised that I would be getting a draft of the offer letter via email and to take one or two days to get back to them.

I immediately contacted my counselor at the non-profit organization, seeking advice and expressing my concerns about not being able to finish the mentorship program if I was to accept the offer. Very calmly she told me not to worry, that the entire purpose of it was to get to this outcome: enabling and accelerating the transition process of newcomers into the job market. She suggested that I accept the offer right away and provide two weeks' notice to my mentor, which was the normal practice.

After I got back to the human resources manager with the signed letter and expected start date, all I had to do was to speak to my mentor and give him the good news as well. For some reason, I was quite nervous about delivering the news to him. I still thought it would be disrespectful to leave the company before the contract finished and not take the three more months' employment extension he offered.

THE AMERICAN DREAM

My mentor was quite shocked and disappointed to hear my news. His silence ended the conversation very rapidly, but before I left his office he asked when my last day would be; that is when I handed him the letter.

That same day, when I was also delivering the news to my friend, my mentor called me into his office once again. To my surprise, he reiterated that I was doing a great job and did not want to see me go. What came next was very gratifying and encouraging; he had an envelope with an offer letter for a full-time position and asked me once more to stay. He explained how great the benefits of the company were and that I would be making more money. He also advised he would not normally do something like this, but he needed someone like me to be part of his team.

I got very excited and could not hide my happiness. I asked for time to think about my options before giving him an answer; I needed to talk to my counselor and ask for advice one more time. When my counselor heard the news, she got very excited as well and asked me to wait couple of hours. She needed to do some research on the companies where the offers were coming from and figure out which one had the most potential for my future.

The next day, she gave me a call to explain the outcome of her research. It turned out that the firm where I was completing the mentorship program had a bigger market cap, future revenue growth projections, and its employees outnumbered the new firm's two to one. On the other hand, the position at the new company was more technically appealing, as I would be applying more of the concepts learned at school, and most importantly, it offered more challenges from a leadership-growth perspective.

Now I had two options to think about: one, stick to my decision of joining the new company or, two, use the second offer to negotiate a higher salary with the current one. I even came up with a third option, which was very risky: I decided to phone the new company to advise that I was being offered a better salary where I was working. They certainly understood my situation and knew this could have probably happened. In fact, right during the phone conversation and without knowing how much I was offered to stay, they beat both, the offer presented by my mentor and their own. It was a no brainer. Although this new opportunity was an entry level position, I felt professionally valued. I confirmed that I was in fact, at the right place at the right time.

Chapter Eleven

New Challenges

Believe in yourself and you will be unstoppable.
~Unknown

Two weeks later I started my new job. The team I would be working with was way bigger than the one I was a part of and everyone was very friendly, but I could not help being nervous. That day I felt the same way my children probably did when they went to school for the very first time. After meeting the entire team, I got to work. My focus, once again, was getting to know the products and services offered by the company, as well as the internal processes and front-line personnel *(people, products, processes)*.

During my first few weeks, the manager I was reporting to display the same great attitude he'd shown during the interview process – giving me the confidence I needed to be me, making me feel part of the team and, most importantly, reassuring me that I would be learning a great deal from him. In no time, the manager also became my mentor, sharing with me some of the experiences he lived when he came to the country, as well as some tips on how to be influential, a better employee and a great leader. I wasted no time and did my part by asking questions and extracting the knowledge I needed to enrich my experience as a professional.

> I was there working with him and his other employees, learning his style and polishing my business acumen.

Another piece of advice I could certainly give is that during any professional or personal journey, no matter where in the world you are, you need to identify leaders and people looking to excel from any perspective, people starving for success. You will soon start to understand their philosophy, thought processes and drive. They will hold your hand, and at the same time push you beyond your boundaries, just because they truly want you to succeed. That is the ultimate goal of a leader: to develop new leaders.

THE AMERICAN DREAM

I rapidly began to demonstrate my capabilities. In the first couple of months, I met the expectations of the role I was hired for, but I would not settle for that – it is not part of my nature. I noticed that my mentor was working really hard and smart to show off his skills and talent to the general manager of the company. He knew it was a matter of time before getting a promotion or a position with more responsibilities. He certainly was not afraid of the challenges given to him, and his confidence in meeting customers and other senior staff deadlines was very impressive.

The great thing about the entire situation was that I was there working with him and his other employees, learning his style and polishing my business acumen and capabilities. I soon realized that it was a matter of time before I was given greater responsibilities as well. I just needed to be patient and wait for the opportunity.

The way I was feeling at that moment proved to me that enthusiasm, positive energy and a good attitude are very contagious, so be careful who you connect yourself with at your workplace and at any personal level.

Every day at the end of the work shift I would stop by my mentor's office and ask how the day had gone – this routine soon evolved into brainstorming sessions about how the business operations could be improved and all the potential the company would have if some of ideas we were discussing could be implemented. I took all the insights and thoughts we had, and in my free time I started to strategically develop a plan where most of the concepts we discussed could be implemented in no time.

It took me approximately a month to develop a robust strategy and implementation plan. I still remember that when I presented the initiative to him, his eyes opened wide in astonishment. I covered every aspect of the business – products, processes and people – from the high-level vision to the line-by-line execution plan. He saw the initiative as that small push he needed to make it into the next level of the organization. Of course, there was some fine-tuning I had to do after he provided his feedback.

Soon enough the area he or "we" were responsible for started to generate positive results to the branch's financials. Productivity and margins were increasing to the point where all other area managers wondered what was being done differently.

One Friday afternoon when I was getting ready to go home, I saw my mentor explaining to the general manager of the company how the plan we created worked. The following Monday, he shared with me some good news: the general manager wanted to expand our strategy to all other areas in the facility and my mentor would be responsible for that implementation. This was something exciting and was the first sign of a promotion coming his way. After I got to my desk and opened my emails, I noticed a message from the general manager thanking me for the ideas and hard work I had put into the new program.

Very quickly our facility started to increase its business results compared to the sister facilities in the city and province. Something I've never forgotten and would encourage everyone to do is to recognize someone else's *smart* work and contributions and never take credit for them; my leader always did that. Every time he had the chance, he would acknowledge that I was, somehow, the mastermind behind some of the success of his department. In one of our conversations he said something to me that after so many years I hope never to forget:

> I realized the time to look for new opportunities and challenges had come.

If I can show my boss that there's someone behind me ready to take my seat and do what I can do, two things could happen: The first one is that if I'm doing a mediocre job, the company could get rid of me without affecting the business – of course, I'll never be mediocre. The second one is the one I always think of: if a better challenge or a promotion comes my way, I could easily be replaced just because someone is ready to take my position, making it easier for my leaders to let me advance. This certainly helps the person behind me follow the same path. I'll call that success.!

That was the start of a good professional relationship. My mentor soon moved into a new role where he became the general manager of another region, giving me the opportunity to take over his role and lead the department he had been responsible for. Soon I started to live and experience what leaders do, I began to develop more people and continued to deliver the results the organization was expecting from our department. I spent approximately six years in the organization, leading other departments and working on regional expansion projects, where I had the chance to meet and work with other great people.

After a while I felt that I was becoming complacent with what I had accomplished thus far, it was like a cycle had restarted. I realized the time to look for new opportunities and challenges had come.

THE AMERICAN DREAM

After many years working for the company, I had not come across many more leaders I could connect with and learn from. As I've mentioned several times in this book, looking up to other leaders was an essential instinct that helped me find more success.

If you have the energy and drive to try new things, please waste no time and go after them! Do not get to the point where you wonder what would have happened if you had made the decision to do it. A word of caution though: if you are going to try something new, make sure it is something <u>bigger and better</u>. I have come across situations where people change jobs just because they did not like a person where they worked or they did not like the way someone behaved towards them; these types of situations are found in every workplace, no matter where you are or the type of organization you work for. So, think and reflect about it before you make a move.

Chapter Twelve

My Secret and My True Dream

The best is yet to come! ~Cy Coleman/Frank Sinatra

Several years later, after working for other companies, I landed a job at one of the best and biggest corporations in the world. It took time, perseverance and patience but the wait was worth it. The experience I gained throughout the years coupled with the education I had made me a good candidate for the type of positions I was looking for. It was not easy, though, as there were many other qualified people applying for these jobs.

I was, somewhat, obsessed with this company, and I decided to do something I'd never done before: cold-calling. I needed my name, resume, application – everything – to stand out. Several times I picked up the phone and called the human resources department to inquire about the job, follow-up with the recruitment process, find out who the hiring manager was, learn more about the skillset they needed, and so forth. And it worked. In one of my many attempts, I got hold of the internal recruiter responsible for filling the position. I was so ready for the job that during our first phone conversation he completed some pre-screening questions, where he learned more about my professional background, education and a few things from my personal life. This facilitated the process for him to set up an interview session with the hiring manager.

> I continued to develop my leadership and influential skills.

The next interview could not have gone any better. The hiring manager stated that he was interested in working with me but also wanted some of his colleagues and the general manager of the business to interview me, as there was another position he believed I would be even more suitable for. In just weeks, I completed six different interviews and was offered a position where I had the chance to work with people from all the different departments and areas of the organization at that location, from the floor sweeper to the general manager and other executives.

After a few years on the job, where I continued to develop my leadership and influential skills and met great leaders and mentors within the organization, I was offered the opportunity to be part of a leadership program where I could complete a master's degree in business and hold positions of increased responsibilities with global scope.

Soon after that, I was offered another leadership position in the USA, where I would have the opportunity to transform the business in a way that I never imagined before, using all the skills and knowledge learned throughout the years in what I called a *true* global leadership role. I became a citizen of the world; I had the opportunity to work in countries where I was not sure what continents they were part of, and I explored cultures I had only heard of in movies or travel magazines. To my satisfaction and with some irony in my words, I am glad I had the chance to close a loop by returning to the USA to do what I do best – the place where I had first tried to pursue my dreams.

Leadership, dedication, and most importantly believing in myself prompted me to accelerate in my career path. You need to find the formula for your own success. You need to look back and take note of all the things that worked best for you. In my case, these things are discipline, dedication, a passion for what I believe and do, and most importantly, family. For you, it could be the same – or even other things such as prosperity, money, power, and so on. It's your call. You need to figure it out for yourself – and time will help you do that.

Success is dependent on you and only you. No one else but you got you to the place or circumstances you are in at this very moment. The good news is that you have the power to steer yourself in the right direction. So start doing it now.

You must also give yourself some ground rules to follow, and most importantly, you need to create a system and operating structure to keep you focused. I did that. For me it was very important to differentiate and understand some key concepts that later became part of my secret formula to continue to move forward.

Leadership, dedication, and most importantly believing in myself prompted me to accelerate in my career path.

My secret is to master the *Science of Achieving* and the *Art of Fulfilling* – even today I am still developing my understating of these two concepts but reflecting about them always keeps me on track. I first heard of these from a great leader, motivator and speaker, Tony Robbins, but I am giving it my own twist and here is how they help me.

If you think about *Achieving*, you need to follow certain steps to reach your goals, but the question depends upon your drive to achieve those goals. Here what you are pursuing is not necessarily linked to a personal desire or satisfaction. That is when *Fulfilling* comes into place. In this case your thoughts and actions are directly linked to your desire and personal satisfaction.

For good or bad, at the early stages of my professional career, I can say that my formula was ~70% achieving and ~20% fulfilling, postponing some personal desires, activities or projects I really wanted to do. As you master the skill of achieving, develop a reputation over time, and prove the type of professional you are, you will have the leverage to balance the formula to +80% achieving and +80% fulfilling, giving you the opportunity to be an achiever but at the same time do what you truly love doing. By the way, perfection would be looking 100% on both.

Understating *Progression* was also part of my system. On very rare occasions you can reach your goals from one day to the next, but you need to take

THE AMERICAN DREAM

massive actions and be disciplined to get there. Here are some examples to relate to from what I heard from another great orator and motivator, Simon Sinek.

Remember when you met your significant other; although there could have been some chemistry at first sight or butterflies in your stomach, you did not look into her/his eyes and say: *I want to spend the rest of my life with you. Would you marry me?* If you did and the answer was yes and you are living a happy life, you should be writing a book about it. You most likely started orchestrating a plan to make her/him fall in love first, right? You started to create some milestones and followed specific actions to make progress towards *Achieving* those milestones: first date, first kiss, meeting mom and dad, moving in together. Later on, you were finally *Fulfilled* when the vows were shared and the "Yes, I do!" was said.

With no doubt in my mind, this is applicable to your professional life; you also need to identify those stepping stones or series of events that will help you keep growing by achieving your goals and fulfilling your dreams. At the end of the day, if you are not fulfilled, you have nothing.

Sitting back and reflecting on my accomplishments and failures, there are a few things,

I lived through – or continue to go through in my everlasting journey – that made me realize my true dream was not fulfilled with monetary compensation or any sort of status in an organization or social setting. My true dream is lived and fulfilled every time I look into my children's eyes and see a bright future ahead of them; when I feel so loved when they look back at me with a wonderful and beautiful smile every time they see my face or hear my voice.

At the end of my journey, I am certain that they will see my hard work as a path already created for them to follow, or as a stepping stone for them to create their own path and pursue their dreams.

When someone says that the sky is the limit they are probably right, but why settle only for the sky? When now we can reach beyond that point and get to places in the universe no one has ever been to before – what's your limit?

And so, the adventure begins…!

A Commitment

This book is about taking action, so I encourage you to reflect and think of three behaviors you believe you are doing great and must continue to do to be successful, as well as three other behaviors you must consider doing moving forward.

I believe in the power of the pen and paper… please write them down.

Continues

1. _____
2. _____
3. _____

Considers

1. _____
2. _____
3. _____

Let's grow together…!

Thanks for taking the time to flip through these pages. I certainly hope you found some inspiration, motivation and/or encouragement to become better leaders, achievers, or people.

If you know someone who is looking for words of encouragement or needs that extra motivation to jump into that next adventure, feel free to give them a copy of this book; the gift of motivation is priceless, and I am certain they will be grateful.

My commitment to individuals or families pursuing their dreams will always be a priority. Please note that part of the proceeds of this book will be invested back to the community and in those who are settling down in a new country.

THE AMERICAN DREAM

Stay connected by leaving an on-line review or providing feedback via Amazon, LinkedIn at: andresgutierrezz, or Twitter at: @DI1o1. If you need me as a speaker or coach, please drop me a line.

Best regards,

Andres Gutierrez, P.Eng., PMP

Toronto, Canada | Houston, Texas

About the author

Andres migrated to North America at a very young age with a bag full of dreams and goals. A non-complacent mentality, perseverance and smart work helped him land leadership positions in big corporations and settle in a new country that he proudly calls home.

www.ingramcontent.com/pod-product-compliance
Lightning Source LLC
Chambersburg PA
CBHW071421210526
45465CB00001B/477